Don't Dream It, OVBE IT!

WEALTH BUDGET PLANNER

Jay K. Porter

OVBE

ISBN-13: 9781952361005

www.ovbe.club

How To Use This Planner

This wealth budget planner is exactly the tool you need to develop a plan for financial freedom, learn how you spend, or keep track of your financial goals.

The key to reaching any financial goal depends on your discipline and organization. Envision your ultimate goal, write it down, and try your best to follow your plan. Treat your finances as if you are the CEO of a fortune 500 company.

Use this planner to save money, track spending habits, stick to a budget, or as a tool to pay down debt. It will help you analyze how your discretionary income increases or decreases based on how you spend, save, or add multiple streams of income.

Understanding the ins and outs of your cash flow, can help you plan to invest in stocks, real estate, build an emergency fund, take a vacation, start a business, or occasionally splurge on luxuries.

The next step is to define your long term goals, and then break them up into smaller steps to be completed over a specific amount of time. Be flexible with your plan and adjust accordingly.

On paper everything seems simple, but life happens. Birthdays, holidays, weddings, gifts, bills, kids, and life emergencies will put a dent in your plan. So plan to adjust and choose how you spend and save wisely.

Thank you for giving this planner a try, best of luck to you with achieving your financial goals, and feel free to reach out to me on social media or join OVBE at www.ovbe.club, and we can encourage each other while we make our dreams a reality.

OVBE @mr_ovbe * Instagram @mr_ovbe * Twitter @mr_ovbe

Wealth Budget

Created By:

Life Goals

Skills I Have

Skills To Learn

Resourceful Websites

Life Goals

Active Income

Passive Income

Business Ideas

Life Goals

Assets Owned

Assets To Acquire

Resourceful Websites

Life Goals

Investments Owned

Investments To Buy

Business Ideas

M
E
M
O
01

Wealth Budget Planner

Monthly Overview

Month: Yr:

Income	Amt.		Income	Amt.	
					Add totals A & B to calculate your total monthly income
Total A		+	Total B		=

Expense	Amt.		Expense	Amt.	
					Add totals C & D to calculate your total monthly expenses
Total C		+	Total D		=

Monthly Income - Monthly Expenses	-	Spend less than you earn and do more with less.	Monthly $100\left(\frac{\text{Expenses}}{\text{Monthly Income}}\right)$	$100\left(\frac{\quad}{\quad}\right)$
Discretionary Income			Debt To Income Ratio %	

Increase your discretionary income by reducing expenses, or generating more income. It is key to saving, investing, and being financially free.

Aim for a debt to income ratio of less <36%. This ratio is an indicator of your default risk. The lower the better.

Wealth Budget Planner

Bill Tracker

Month: Yr:

Bill	Amt. Due	Due Date	Amt. Paid	Paid Date	Paid On Time
					Yes No
					Yes No
					Yes No
					Yes No
					Yes No
					Yes No
					Yes No
					Yes No
					Yes No
					Yes No
					Yes No
					Yes No
					Yes No
					Yes No
					Yes No
					Yes No
					Yes No
					Yes No
					Yes No
					Yes No
					Yes No
					Yes No
					Yes No
					Yes No

Wealth Budget Planner

Calendar

Month: Yr:

	Sunday	Monday	Tuesday	Wednesday	Thursday	Friday	Saturday
Save Invest Build							
Dream Plan Live							
Save Invest Build							
Dream Plan Live							
Save Invest Build							

Notes & Reminders

Special occasions, Items to buy, Appointments, & To Do Lists

Weekly Spending Tracker

Wk.#

/ / S M T W TH F S	
Add all columns for Daily Total:	

/ / S M T W TH F S	
Add all columns for Daily Total:	

/ / S M T W TH F S	
Add all columns for Daily Total:	

/ / S M T W TH F S	
Add all columns for Daily Total:	

Wealth Budget Planner

Weekly Spending Tracker

Wk.#

/ / S M T W TH F S	
Add all columns for Daily Total:	

/ / S M T W TH F S	
Add all columns for Daily Total:	

/ / S M T W TH F S	
Add all columns for Daily Total:	

/ - / Week End Totals

Sun.	
Mon.	
Tues.	
Wed.	
Thurs.	
Fri.	
Sat.	
Week Total:	

How much did you save this week?

Is there extra to invest?

List your week total and money saved on the monthly budget tracker.

Think of ways to cut back on unnecessary spending, or how to spend more efficiently.

Wealth Budget Planner

Weekly Spending Tracker

Wk.#

/ / S M T W TH F S	
Add all columns for Daily Total:	

/ / S M T W TH F S	
Add all columns for Daily Total:	

/ / S M T W TH F S	
Add all columns for Daily Total:	

/ / S M T W TH F S	
Add all columns for Daily Total:	

Wealth Budget Planner

Weekly Spending Tracker

Wk.#

/ / S M T W TH F S	
Add all columns for Daily Total:	

/ / S M T W TH F S	
Add all columns for Daily Total:	

/ / S M T W TH F S	
Add all columns for Daily Total:	

/ - /	Week End Totals
Sun.	
Mon.	
Tues.	
Wed.	
Thurs.	
Fri.	
Sat.	
Week Total:	

How much did you save this week?

Is there extra to invest?

List your week total and money saved on the monthly budget tracker.

Think of ways to cut back on unnecessary spending, or how to spend more efficiently.

Wealth Budget Planner

Weekly Spending Tracker

Wk.#

/ / S M T W TH F S	
Add all columns for Daily Total:	

/ / S M T W TH F S	
Add all columns for Daily Total:	

/ / S M T W TH F S	
Add all columns for Daily Total:	

/ / S M T W TH F S	
Add all columns for Daily Total:	

Wealth Budget Planner

Weekly Spending Tracker

Wk.#

/ / S M T W TH F S	

Add all columns for
Daily Total:

/ / S M T W TH F S	

Add all columns for
Daily Total:

/ / S M T W TH F S	

Add all columns for
Daily Total:

/ - / Week End Totals

Sun.	
Mon.	
Tues.	
Wed.	
Thurs.	
Fri.	
Sat.	
Week Total:	

How much did you save this week?

Is there extra to invest?

List your week total and money saved on the monthly budget tracker.

Think of ways to cut back on unnecessary spending, or how to spend more efficiently.

Wealth Budget Planner

Weekly Spending Tracker

Wk.#

/ / S M T W TH F S

ADD ALL COLUMNS FOR
DAILY TOTAL:

/ / S M T W TH F S

ADD ALL COLUMNS FOR
DAILY TOTAL:

/ / S M T W TH F S

ADD ALL COLUMNS FOR
DAILY TOTAL:

/ / S M T W TH F S

ADD ALL COLUMNS FOR
DAILY TOTAL:

Wealth Budget Planner

Weekly Spending Tracker

Wk.#

/ / S M T W TH F S	
Add all columns for Daily Total:	

/ / S M T W TH F S	
Add all columns for Daily Total:	

/ / S M T W TH F S	
Add all columns for Daily Total:	

/ - / Week End Totals

Sun.	
Mon.	
Tues.	
Wed.	
Thurs.	
Fri.	
Sat.	
Week Total:	

How much did you save this week?

Is there extra to invest?

List your week total and money saved on the monthly budget tracker.

Think of ways to cut back on unnecessary spending, or how to spend more efficiently.

Wealth Budget Planner

Weekly Spending Tracker

Wk.#

/ / S M T W TH F S	
Add all columns for Daily Total:	

/ / S M T W TH F S	
Add all columns for Daily Total:	

/ / S M T W TH F S	
Add all columns for Daily Total:	

/ / S M T W TH F S	
Add all columns for Daily Total:	

Wealth Budget Planner

Weekly Spending Tracker

Wk.#

/ / S M T W TH F S	
Add all columns for Daily Total:	

/ / S M T W TH F S	
Add all columns for Daily Total:	

/ / S M T W TH F S	
Add all columns for Daily Total:	

/ - /	Week End Totals
Sun.	
Mon.	
Tues.	
Wed.	
Thurs.	
Fri.	
Sat.	
Week Total:	

How much did you save this week?

Is there extra to invest?

List your week total and money saved on the monthly budget tracker.

Think of ways to cut back on unnecessary spending, or how to spend more efficiently.

Wealth Budget Planner

Monthly Budget Tracker

Subtract your week end totals from your discretionary income	
Discretionary Income	
Week 1.	
Week 2.	
Week 3.	
Week 4.	
Week 5.	
Surplus Cash:	

Savings
Add savings 1-5 for total savings
1.
2.
3.
4.
5.
Total Savings:

"Live below your means but within your needs."

Suze Orman

Budget Check

Are you spending more or less than planned for the month?

Are you happy with your surplus amount of cash?

Did you meet your savings goal for the month?

Are there expenses that could be reduced or eliminated, by a change in behavior?

Did you generate any extra income?

Think of some things you can do to increase your surplus cash and write them down.

Every month you should learn something new or perfect an existing skill, research assets to acquire, invest in stocks, and focus on creating income streams. Create a habit of success. Strike through all that apply during this month.

Researched Assets	Read a book	Perfected a skill
Invested in stocks	Thought of new income streams	Set new goals
Learned a new Skill	Wrote Down Ideas	Relaxed

If missed anything you wanted to do, be honest and write down what stopped you. Try your best to remove or change obstacles that stifle your success.

FINANCIAL STRATEGIES & CALCULATIONS

SAVINGS GOALS, CUTBACKS, INVESTING, FORMULAS, & STRATEGIES

Wealth Budget Planner

Financial Strategies & Calculations

Savings Goals, Cutbacks, Investing, Formulas, & Strategies

M
E
M
O
02

THE UNITED STATES OF AMERIC
ONE DOLLAR
G88969823G
WASHINGTON,D.C.
THIS NOTE IS LEGAL TENDER FOR ALL DEBTS, PUBLIC AND PRIVATE
THE UNITED S
NOTE
ERICA

Wealth Budget Planner

Monthly Overview

Month: Yr:

Income	Amt.		Income	Amt.	
					Add totals A & B to calculate your total monthly income
Total A		+	Total B		=

Expense	Amt.		Expense	Amt.	
					Add totals C & D to calculate your total monthly expenses
Total C		+	Total D		=

Monthly Income - Monthly Expenses	-	Spend less than you earn and do more with less.	$100\left(\frac{\text{Expenses}}{\text{Monthly Income}}\right)$	$100\left(\frac{\quad}{\quad}\right)$
Discretionary Income			Debt To Income Ratio %	

Increase your discretionary income by reducing expenses, or generating more income. It is key to saving, investing, and being financially free.

Aim for a debt to income ratio of less <36%. This ratio is an indicator of your default risk. The lower the better.

Bill Tracker

Month: Yr:

Bill	Amt. Due	Due Date	Amt. Paid	Paid Date	Paid On Time
					Yes No
					Yes No
					Yes No
					Yes No
					Yes No
					Yes No
					Yes No
					Yes No
					Yes No
					Yes No
					Yes No
					Yes No
					Yes No
					Yes No
					Yes No
					Yes No
					Yes No
					Yes No
					Yes No
					Yes No
					Yes No
					Yes No
					Yes No
					Yes No

Wealth Budget Planner

Calendar

Month: Yr:

	Sunday	Monday	Tuesday	Wednesday	Thursday	Friday	Saturday
Save Invest Build							
Dream Plan Live							
Save Invest Build							
Dream Plan Live							
Save Invest Build							

Notes & Reminders

Special occasions, Items to buy, Appointments, & To Do Lists

WEALTH BUDGET PLANNER

WEEKLY SPENDING TRACKER

WK.#

/ / S M T W TH F S	
ADD ALL COLUMNS FOR DAILY TOTAL:	

/ / S M T W TH F S	
ADD ALL COLUMNS FOR DAILY TOTAL:	

/ / S M T W TH F S	
ADD ALL COLUMNS FOR DAILY TOTAL:	

/ / S M T W TH F S	
ADD ALL COLUMNS FOR DAILY TOTAL:	

Wealth Budget Planner

Weekly Spending Tracker

Wk.#

/ / S M T W TH F S	
Add all columns for Daily Total:	

/ / S M T W TH F S	
Add all columns for Daily Total:	

/ / S M T W TH F S	
Add all columns for Daily Total:	

/ - /	Week End Totals
Sun.	
Mon.	
Tues.	
Wed.	
Thurs.	
Fri.	
Sat.	
Week Total:	

How much did you save this week?

Is there extra to invest?

List your week total and money saved on the monthly budget tracker.

Think of ways to cut back on unnecessary spending, or how to spend more efficiently.

Wealth Budget Planner

Weekly Spending Tracker

Wk.#

/ / S M T W TH F S	

Add all columns for
Daily Total:

/ / S M T W TH F S	

Add all columns for
Daily Total:

/ / S M T W TH F S	

Add all columns for
Daily Total:

/ / S M T W TH F S	

Add all columns for
Daily Total:

Wealth Budget Planner

Weekly Spending Tracker

Wk.#

/ / S M T W TH F S	
Add all columns for Daily Total:	

/ / S M T W TH F S	
Add all columns for Daily Total:	

/ / S M T W TH F S	
Add all columns for Daily Total:	

/ - / Week End Totals

Sun.	
Mon.	
Tues.	
Wed.	
Thurs.	
Fri.	
Sat.	
Week Total:	

How much did you save this week?

Is there extra to invest?

List your week total and money saved on the monthly budget tracker.

Think of ways to cut back on unnecessary spending, or how to spend more efficiently.

Wealth Budget Planner

Weekly Spending Tracker

Wk.#

/ / S M T W TH F S

Add all columns for
Daily Total:

/ / S M T W TH F S

Add all columns for
Daily Total:

/ / S M T W TH F S

Add all columns for
Daily Total:

/ / S M T W TH F S

Add all columns for
Daily Total:

Wealth Budget Planner

Weekly Spending Tracker

Wk.#

/ / S M T W TH F S	
Add all columns for Daily Total:	

/ / S M T W TH F S	
Add all columns for Daily Total:	

/ / S M T W TH F S	
Add all columns for Daily Total:	

/ - /	Week End Totals
Sun.	
Mon.	
Tues.	
Wed.	
Thurs.	
Fri.	
Sat.	
Week Total:	

How much did you save this week?

Is there extra to invest?

List your week total and money saved on the monthly budget tracker.

Think of ways to cut back on unnecessary spending, or how to spend more efficiently.

Wealth Budget Planner

Weekly Spending Tracker

Wk.#

/ / S M T W TH F S

Add all columns for
Daily Total:

/ / S M T W TH F S

Add all columns for
Daily Total:

/ / S M T W TH F S

Add all columns for
Daily Total:

/ / S M T W TH F S

Add all columns for
Daily Total:

Wealth Budget Planner

Weekly Spending Tracker

Wk.#

/ / S M T W TH F S	
Add all columns for **Daily Total:**	

/ / S M T W TH F S	
Add all columns for **Daily Total:**	

/ / S M T W TH F S	
Add all columns for **Daily Total:**	

/ - /	Week End Totals
Sun.	
Mon.	
Tues.	
Wed.	
Thurs.	
Fri.	
Sat.	
Week Total:	

How much did you save this week?

Is there extra to invest?

List your week total and money saved on the monthly budget tracker.

Think of ways to cut back on unnecessary spending, or how to spend more efficiently.

Wealth Budget Planner

Weekly Spending Tracker

Wk.#

/ / S M T W TH F S	
Add all columns for Daily Total:	

/ / S M T W TH F S	
Add all columns for Daily Total:	

/ / S M T W TH F S	
Add all columns for Daily Total:	

/ / S M T W TH F S	
Add all columns for Daily Total:	

Wealth Budget Planner

Weekly Spending Tracker

Wk.#

/ / S M T W TH F S	
Add all columns for Daily Total:	

/ / S M T W TH F S	
Add all columns for Daily Total:	

/ / S M T W TH F S	
Add all columns for Daily Total:	

/ - / Week End Totals

Sun.	
Mon.	
Tues.	
Wed.	
Thurs.	
Fri.	
Sat.	
Week Total:	

How much did you save this week?

Is there extra to invest?

List your week total and money saved on the monthly budget tracker.

Think of ways to cut back on unnecessary spending, or how to spend more efficiently.

Wealth Budget Planner

Monthly Budget Tracker

Subtract your week end totals from your discretionary income	
Discretionary Income	
Week 1.	
Week 2.	
Week 3.	
Week 4.	
Week 5.	
Surplus Cash:	

Savings
Add savings 1-5 for total savings
1.
2.
3.
4.
5.
Total Savings:

"You've got to tell your money what to do or it will leave you."

Dave Ramsey

Budget Check

Are you spending more or less than planned for the month?

Are you happy with your surplus amount of cash?

Did you meet your savings goal for the month?

Are there expenses that could be reduced or eliminated, by a change in behavior?

Did you generate any extra income?

Think of some things you can do to increase your surplus cash and write them down.

Every month you should learn something new or perfect an existing skill, research assets to acquire, invest in stocks, and focus on creating income streams. Create a habit of success. Strike through all that apply during this month.

Researched Assets	Read a book	Perfected a skill
Invested in stocks	Thought of new income streams	Set new goals
Learned a new skill	Wrote Down Ideas	Relaxed

If missed anything you wanted to do, be honest and write down what stopped you. Try your best to remove or change obstacles that stifle your success.

Financial Strategies & Calculations

Savings Goals, Cutbacks, Investing, Formulas, & Strategies

Financial Strategies & Calculations

Savings Goals, Cutbacks, Investing, Formulas, & Strategies

MEMO 03

Wealth Budget Planner

Monthly Overview

Month: Yr:

Income	Amt.		Income	Amt.	
					Add totals A & B to calculate your total monthly income
Total A		+	Total B		=

Expense	Amt.		Expense	Amt.	
					Add totals C & D to calculate your total monthly expenses
Total C		+	Total D		=

Monthly Income - Monthly Expenses	-	Spend less than you earn and do more with less.	100 (Monthly Expenses / Monthly Income)	100( )
Discretionary Income			Debt To Income Ratio %	

Increase your discretionary income by reducing expenses, or generating more income. It is key to saving, investing, and being financially free.

Aim for a debt to income ratio of less <36%. This ratio is an indicator of your default risk. The lower the better.

BILL TRACKER

MONTH: YR:

BILL	AMT. DUE	DUE DATE	AMT. PAID	PAID DATE	PAID ON TIME
					YES NO
					YES NO
					YES NO
					YES NO
					YES NO
					YES NO
					YES NO
					YES NO
					YES NO
					YES NO
					YES NO
					YES NO
					YES NO
					YES NO
					YES NO
					YES NO
					YES NO
					YES NO
					YES NO
					YES NO
					YES NO
					YES NO
					YES NO
					YES NO

Wealth Budget Planner

Calendar

Month: **Yr:**

	Sunday	Monday	Tuesday	Wednesday	Thursday	Friday	Saturday
Save Invest Build							
Dream Plan Live							
Save Invest Build							
Dream Plan Live							
Save Invest Build							

Notes & Reminders

Special occasions, Items to buy, Appointments, & To Do Lists

Wealth Budget Planner

Weekly Spending Tracker

Wk.#

/ / S M T W TH F S	
Add all columns for **Daily Total:**	

/ / S M T W TH F S	
Add all columns for **Daily Total:**	

/ / S M T W TH F S	
Add all columns for **Daily Total:**	

/ / S M T W TH F S	
Add all columns for **Daily Total:**	

Wealth Budget Planner

Weekly Spending Tracker

Wk.#

/ / S M T W TH F S	

Add all columns for
Daily Total:

/ / S M T W TH F S	

Add all columns for
Daily Total:

/ / S M T W TH F S	

Add all columns for
Daily Total:

/ - / Week End Totals

Sun.	
Mon.	
Tues.	
Wed.	
Thurs.	
Fri.	
Sat.	
Week Total:	

How much did you save this week?

Is there extra to invest?

List your week total and money saved on the monthly budget tracker.

Think of ways to cut back on unnecessary spending, or how to spend more efficiently.

Wealth Budget Planner

Weekly Spending Tracker

Wk.#

/ / S M T W TH F S	

Add all columns for
Daily Total:

/ / S M T W TH F S	

Add all columns for
Daily Total:

/ / S M T W TH F S	

Add all columns for
Daily Total:

/ / S M T W TH F S	

Add all columns for
Daily Total:

Wealth Budget Planner

Weekly Spending Tracker

Wk.#

/ / S M T W TH F S	
Add all columns for Daily Total:	

/ / S M T W TH F S	
Add all columns for Daily Total:	

/ / S M T W TH F S	
Add all columns for Daily Total:	

/ - / Week End Totals

Sun.	
Mon.	
Tues.	
Wed.	
Thurs.	
Fri.	
Sat.	
Week Total:	

How much did you save this week?

Is there extra to invest?

List your week total and money saved on the monthly budget tracker.

Think of ways to cut back on unnecessary spending, or how to spend more efficiently.

Wealth Budget Planner

Weekly Spending Tracker

Wk.#

/ / S M T W TH F S

Add all columns for
Daily Total:

/ / S M T W TH F S

Add all columns for
Daily Total:

/ / S M T W TH F S

Add all columns for
Daily Total:

/ / S M T W TH F S

Add all columns for
Daily Total:

Wealth Budget Planner

Weekly Spending Tracker

Wk.#

/ / S M T W TH F S	
Add all columns for Daily Total:	

/ / S M T W TH F S	
Add all columns for Daily Total:	

/ / S M T W TH F S	
Add all columns for Daily Total:	

/ - / Week End Totals

Sun.	
Mon.	
Tues.	
Wed.	
Thurs.	
Fri.	
Sat.	
Week Total:	

How much did you save this week?

Is there extra to invest?

List your week total and money saved on the monthly budget tracker.

Think of ways to cut back on unnecessary spending, or how to spend more efficiently.

Wealth Budget Planner

Weekly Spending Tracker

Wk.#

/ / S M T W TH F S	
Add all columns for Daily Total:	

/ / S M T W TH F S	
Add all columns for Daily Total:	

/ / S M T W TH F S	
Add all columns for Daily Total:	

/ / S M T W TH F S	
Add all columns for Daily Total:	

Wealth Budget Planner

Weekly Spending Tracker

Wk.#

/ /	S M T W TH F S

Add all columns for
Daily Total:

/ /	S M T W TH F S

Add all columns for
Daily Total:

/ /	S M T W TH F S

Add all columns for
Daily Total:

/ - / Week End Totals

Sun.	
Mon.	
Tues.	
Wed.	
Thurs.	
Fri.	
Sat.	
Week Total:	

How much did you save this week?

Is there extra to invest?

List your week total and money saved on the monthly budget tracker.

Think of ways to cut back on unnecessary spending, or how to spend more efficiently.

WEALTH BUDGET PLANNER

WEEKLY SPENDING TRACKER

WK.#

/ /	S M T W TH F S
ADD ALL COLUMNS FOR DAILY TOTAL:	

/ /	S M T W TH F S
ADD ALL COLUMNS FOR DAILY TOTAL:	

/ /	S M T W TH F S
ADD ALL COLUMNS FOR DAILY TOTAL:	

/ /	S M T W TH F S
ADD ALL COLUMNS FOR DAILY TOTAL:	

Wealth Budget Planner

Weekly Spending Tracker

Wk.#

/ / S M T W TH F S	
Add all columns for Daily Total:	

/ / S M T W TH F S	
Add all columns for Daily Total:	

/ / S M T W TH F S	
Add all columns for Daily Total:	

/ - / Week End Totals

Sun.	
Mon.	
Tues.	
Wed.	
Thurs.	
Fri.	
Sat.	
Week Total:	

How much did you save this week?

Is there extra to invest?

List your week total and money saved on the monthly budget tracker.

Think of ways to cut back on unnecessary spending, or how to spend more efficiently.

Wealth Budget Planner

Monthly Budget Tracker

Subtract your week end totals from your discretionary income	
Discretionary Income	
Week 1.	
Week 2.	
Week 3.	
Week 4.	
Week 5.	
Surplus Cash:	

Savings
Add savings 1-5 for total savings
1.
2.
3.
4.
5.
Total Savings:

"Measure your wealth by what you'd have left if you lost all of your money."

H. Jackson Brown Jr.

Budget Check

Are you spending more or less than planned for the month?

Are you happy with your surplus amount of cash?

Did you meet your savings goal for the month?

Are there expenses that could be reduced or eliminated, by a change in behavior?

Did you generate any extra income?

Think of some things you can do to increase your surplus cash and write them down.

Every month you should learn something new or perfect an existing skill, research assets to acquire, invest in stocks, and focus on creating income streams. Create a habit of success. Strike through all that apply during this month.

Researched Assets

Read a book

Perfected a skill

Invested in stocks

Thought of new income streams

Set new goals

Learned a new skill

Wrote Down Ideas

Relaxed

If missed anything you wanted to do, be honest and write down what stopped you. Try your best to remove or change obstacles that stifle your success.

FINANCIAL STRATEGIES & CALCULATIONS

SAVINGS GOALS, CUTBACKS, INVESTING, FORMULAS, & STRATEGIES

FINANCIAL STRATEGIES & CALCULATIONS

SAVINGS GOALS, CUTBACKS, INVESTING, FORMULAS, & STRATEGIES

MEMO 04

WEALTH BUDGET PLANNER

MONTHLY OVERVIEW

MONTH: YR:

INCOME	AMT.		INCOME	AMT.	
					Add totals A & B to calculate your total monthly income
TOTAL A		+	TOTAL B		=

EXPENSE	AMT.		EXPENSE	AMT.	
					Add totals C & D to calculate your total monthly expenses
TOTAL C		+	TOTAL D		=

MONTHLY INCOME - MONTHLY EXPENSES	-	Spend less than you earn and do more with less.	$100\left(\frac{\text{MONTHLY EXPENSES}}{\text{MONTHLY INCOME}}\right)$	100(———)
DISCRETIONARY INCOME			DEBT TO INCOME RATIO %	

Increase your discretionary income by reducing expenses, or generating more income. It is key to saving, investing, and being financially free.

Aim for a debt to income ratio of less <36%. This ratio is an indicator of your default risk. The lower the better.

BILL TRACKER

MONTH: YR:

BILL	AMT. DUE	DUE DATE	AMT. PAID	PAID DATE	PAID ON TIME
					YES NO
					YES NO
					YES NO
					YES NO
					YES NO
					YES NO
					YES NO
					YES NO
					YES NO
					YES NO
					YES NO
					YES NO
					YES NO
					YES NO
					YES NO
					YES NO
					YES NO
					YES NO
					YES NO
					YES NO
					YES NO
					YES NO
					YES NO
					YES NO

Wealth Budget Planner

Calendar

Month: Yr:

	Sunday	Monday	Tuesday	Wednesday	Thursday	Friday	Saturday
Save Invest Build							
Dream Plan Live							
Save Invest Build							
Dream Plan Live							
Save Invest Build							

Notes & Reminders

Special occasions, Items to buy, Appointments, & To Do Lists

Wealth Budget Planner

Weekly Spending Tracker

Wk.#

/ / S M T W TH F S	
Add all columns for Daily Total:	

/ / S M T W TH F S	
Add all columns for Daily Total:	

/ / S M T W TH F S	
Add all columns for Daily Total:	

/ / S M T W TH F S	
Add all columns for Daily Total:	

Wealth Budget Planner

Weekly Spending Tracker

Wk.#

/ / S M T W TH F S	
Add all columns for Daily Total:	

/ / S M T W TH F S	
Add all columns for Daily Total:	

/ / S M T W TH F S	
Add all columns for Daily Total:	

/ - /	Week End Totals
Sun.	
Mon.	
Tues.	
Wed.	
Thurs.	
Fri.	
Sat.	
Week Total:	

How much did you save this week?

Is there extra to invest?

List your week total and money saved on the monthly budget tracker.

Think of ways to cut back on unnecessary spending, or how to spend more efficiently.

Wealth Budget Planner

Weekly Spending Tracker

Wk.#

/ / S M T W TH F S	
Add all columns for Daily Total:	

/ / S M T W TH F S	
Add all columns for Daily Total:	

/ / S M T W TH F S	
Add all columns for Daily Total:	

/ / S M T W TH F S	
Add all columns for Daily Total:	

Wealth Budget Planner

Weekly Spending Tracker

Wk.#

/ / S M T W TH F S	
Add all columns for Daily Total:	

/ / S M T W TH F S	
Add all columns for Daily Total:	

/ / S M T W TH F S	
Add all columns for Daily Total:	

/ - / Week End Totals

Sun.	
Mon.	
Tues.	
Wed.	
Thurs.	
Fri.	
Sat.	
Week Total:	

How much did you save this week?

Is there extra to invest?

List your week total and money saved on the monthly budget tracker.

Think of ways to cut back on unnecessary spending, or how to spend more efficiently.

Wealth Budget Planner

Weekly Spending Tracker

Wk.#

/ / S M T W TH F S	
Add all columns for Daily Total:	

/ / S M T W TH F S	
Add all columns for Daily Total:	

/ / S M T W TH F S	
Add all columns for Daily Total:	

/ / S M T W TH F S	
Add all columns for Daily Total:	

Wealth Budget Planner

Weekly Spending Tracker

Wk.#

/ / S M T W TH F S	
Add all columns for Daily Total:	

/ / S M T W TH F S	
Add all columns for Daily Total:	

/ / S M T W TH F S	
Add all columns for Daily Total:	

/ - /	Week End Totals
Sun.	
Mon.	
Tues.	
Wed.	
Thurs.	
Fri.	
Sat.	
Week Total:	

How much did you save this week?

Is there extra to invest?

List your week total and money saved on the monthly budget tracker.

Think of ways to cut back on unnecessary spending, or how to spend more efficiently.

Weekly Spending Tracker

Wk.#

/ / S M T W TH F S	
Add all columns for Daily Total:	

/ / S M T W TH F S	
Add all columns for Daily Total:	

/ / S M T W TH F S	
Add all columns for Daily Total:	

/ / S M T W TH F S	
Add all columns for Daily Total:	

Wealth Budget Planner

Weekly Spending Tracker

Wk.#

/ / S M T W TH F S	
Add all columns for Daily Total:	

/ / S M T W TH F S	
Add all columns for Daily Total:	

/ / S M T W TH F S	
Add all columns for Daily Total:	

/ - /	Week End Totals
Sun.	
Mon.	
Tues.	
Wed.	
Thurs.	
Fri.	
Sat.	
Week Total:	

How much did you save this week?

Is there extra to invest?

List your week total and money saved on the monthly budget tracker.

Think of ways to cut back on unnecessary spending, or how to spend more efficiently.

Wealth Budget Planner

Weekly Spending Tracker

Wk.#

/ / S M T W TH F S	

Add all columns for
Daily Total:

/ / S M T W TH F S	

Add all columns for
Daily Total:

/ / S M T W TH F S	

Add all columns for
Daily Total:

/ / S M T W TH F S	

Add all columns for
Daily Total:

WEALTH BUDGET PLANNER

WEEKLY SPENDING TRACKER

WK.#

/ / S M T W TH F S	
ADD ALL COLUMNS FOR DAILY TOTAL:	

/ / S M T W TH F S	
ADD ALL COLUMNS FOR DAILY TOTAL:	

/ / S M T W TH F S	
ADD ALL COLUMNS FOR DAILY TOTAL:	

/ - /		WEEK END TOTALS
SUN.		HOW MUCH DID YOU SAVE THIS WEEK?
MON.		
TUES.		----------------------
WED.		IS THERE EXTRA TO INVEST?
THURS.		
FRI.		LIST YOUR WEEK TOTAL AND MONEY SAVED ON THE MONTHLY BUDGET TRACKER.
SAT.		
WEEK TOTAL:		

THINK OF WAYS TO CUT BACK ON UNNECESSARY SPENDING, OR HOW TO SPEND MORE EFFICIENTLY.

Wealth Budget Planner

Monthly Budget Tracker

Subtract your week end totals from your discretionary income	
Discretionary Income	
Week 1.	
Week 2.	
Week 3.	
Week 4.	
Week 5.	
Surplus Cash:	

Savings
Add savings 1-5 for total savings
1.
2.
3.
4.
5.
Total Savings:

"Build confidence completing easy tasks, so difficult tasks feel like business as usual."

Jay Porter

Budget Check

Are you spending more or less than planned for the month?

Are you happy with your surplus amount of cash?

Did you meet your savings goal for the month?

Are there expenses that could be reduced or eliminated, by a change in behavior?

Did you generate any extra income?

Think of some things you can do to increase your surplus cash and write them down.

Every month you should learn something new or perfect an existing skill, research assets to acquire, invest in stocks, and focus on creating income streams. Create a habit of success. Strike through all that apply during this month.

- Researched Assets
- Invested in stocks
- Learned a new Skill
- Read a book
- Thought of new income streams
- Wrote Down Ideas
- Perfected a skill
- Set new goals
- Relaxed

If missed anything you wanted to do, be honest and write down what stopped you. Try your best to remove or change obstacles that stifle your success.

Financial Strategies & Calculations

Savings Goals, Cutbacks, Investing, Formulas, & Strategies

FINANCIAL STRATEGIES & CALCULATIONS

SAVINGS GOALS, CUTBACKS, INVESTING, FORMULAS, & STRATEGIES

MEMO 05

Wealth Budget Planner

Monthly Overview

Month: Yr:

Income	Amt.		Income	Amt.	
					Add totals A & B to calculate your total monthly income
Total A		+	Total B		=

Expense	Amt.		Expense	Amt.	
					Add totals C & D to calculate your total monthly expenses
Total C		+	Total D		=

Monthly Income - Monthly Expenses	-
Discretionary Income	

Spend less than you earn and do more with less.

Monthly $100\left(\frac{\text{Expenses}}{\text{Monthly Income}}\right)$	$100\left(\text{\_\_\_\_\_\_}\right)$
Debt To Income Ratio %	

Increase your discretionary income by reducing expenses, or generating more income. It is key to saving, investing, and being financially free.

Aim for a debt to income ratio of less <36%. This ratio is an indicator of your default risk. The lower the better.

Bill Tracker

Month: Yr:

Bill	Amt. Due	Due Date	Amt. Paid	Paid Date	Paid On Time
					Yes No
					Yes No
					Yes No
					Yes No
					Yes No
					Yes No
					Yes No
					Yes No
					Yes No
					Yes No
					Yes No
					Yes No
					Yes No
					Yes No
					Yes No
					Yes No
					Yes No
					Yes No
					Yes No
					Yes No
					Yes No
					Yes No
					Yes No
					Yes No

Wealth Budget Planner

Calendar

Month: Yr:

	Sunday	Monday	Tuesday	Wednesday	Thursday	Friday	Saturday
Save Invest Build							
Dream Plan Live							
Save Invest Build							
Dream Plan Live							
Save Invest Build							

Notes & Reminders

Special occasions, Items to buy, Appointments, & To Do Lists

Wealth Budget Planner

Weekly Spending Tracker

Wk.#

/ / S M T W TH F S	
Add all columns for Daily Total:	

/ / S M T W TH F S	
Add all columns for Daily Total:	

/ / S M T W TH F S	
Add all columns for Daily Total:	

/ / S M T W TH F S	
Add all columns for Daily Total:	

Wealth Budget Planner

Weekly Spending Tracker

Wk.#

/ / S M T W TH F S	
Add all columns for Daily Total:	

/ / S M T W TH F S	
Add all columns for Daily Total:	

/ / S M T W TH F S	
Add all columns for Daily Total:	

/ - / Week End Totals

Sun.	
Mon.	
Tues.	
Wed.	
Thurs.	
Fri.	
Sat.	
Week Total:	

How much did you save this week?

Is there extra to invest?

List your week total and money saved on the monthly budget tracker.

Think of ways to cut back on unnecessary spending, or how to spend more efficiently.

Wealth Budget Planner

Weekly Spending Tracker

Wk.#

/ / S M T W TH F S	

Add all columns for
Daily Total:

/ / S M T W TH F S	

Add all columns for
Daily Total:

/ / S M T W TH F S	

Add all columns for
Daily Total:

/ / S M T W TH F S	

Add all columns for
Daily Total:

Wealth Budget Planner

Weekly Spending Tracker

Wk.#

/ / S M T W TH F S	
Add all columns for Daily Total:	

/ / S M T W TH F S	
Add all columns for Daily Total:	

/ / S M T W TH F S	
Add all columns for Daily Total:	

/ - / Week End Totals

Sun.	
Mon.	
Tues.	
Wed.	
Thurs.	
Fri.	
Sat.	
Week Total:	

How much did you save this week?

Is there extra to invest?

List your week total and money saved on the monthly budget tracker.

Think of ways to cut back on unnecessary spending, or how to spend more efficiently.

Weekly Spending Tracker

Wk.#

/ / S M T W TH F S

Add all columns for
Daily Total:

/ / S M T W TH F S

Add all columns for
Daily Total:

/ / S M T W TH F S

Add all columns for
Daily Total:

/ / S M T W TH F S

Add all columns for
Daily Total:

WEALTH BUDGET PLANNER

WEEKLY SPENDING TRACKER

WK.#

/ / S M T W TH F S	
ADD ALL COLUMNS FOR DAILY TOTAL:	

/ / S M T W TH F S	
ADD ALL COLUMNS FOR DAILY TOTAL:	

/ / S M T W TH F S	
ADD ALL COLUMNS FOR DAILY TOTAL:	

/ - / WEEK END TOTALS

SUN.	
MON.	
TUES.	
WED.	
THURS.	
FRI.	
SAT.	
WEEK TOTAL:	

HOW MUCH DID YOU SAVE THIS WEEK?

IS THERE EXTRA TO INVEST?

LIST YOUR WEEK TOTAL AND MONEY SAVED ON THE MONTHLY BUDGET TRACKER.

THINK OF WAYS TO CUT BACK ON UNNECESSARY SPENDING, OR HOW TO SPEND MORE EFFICIENTLY.

Wealth Budget Planner

Weekly Spending Tracker

Wk.#

/ / S M T W TH F S

Add all columns for
Daily Total:

/ / S M T W TH F S

Add all columns for
Daily Total:

/ / S M T W TH F S

Add all columns for
Daily Total:

/ / S M T W TH F S

Add all columns for
Daily Total:

Wealth Budget Planner

Weekly Spending Tracker

Wk.#

/ / S M T W TH F S	
Add all columns for Daily Total:	

/ / S M T W TH F S	
Add all columns for Daily Total:	

/ / S M T W TH F S	
Add all columns for Daily Total:	

/ - / Week End Totals

Sun.	
Mon.	
Tues.	
Wed.	
Thurs.	
Fri.	
Sat.	
Week Total:	

How much did you save this week?

Is there extra to invest?

List your week total and money saved on the monthly budget tracker.

Think of ways to cut back on unnecessary spending, or how to spend more efficiently.

WEALTH BUDGET PLANNER

WEEKLY SPENDING TRACKER

WK.#

/ /	S M T W TH F S
ADD ALL COLUMNS FOR DAILY TOTAL:	

/ /	S M T W TH F S
ADD ALL COLUMNS FOR DAILY TOTAL:	

/ /	S M T W TH F S
ADD ALL COLUMNS FOR DAILY TOTAL:	

/ /	S M T W TH F S
ADD ALL COLUMNS FOR DAILY TOTAL:	

WEALTH BUDGET PLANNER

WEEKLY SPENDING TRACKER

WK.#

/ / S M T W TH F S	

ADD ALL COLUMNS FOR
DAILY TOTAL:

/ / S M T W TH F S	

ADD ALL COLUMNS FOR
DAILY TOTAL:

/ / S M T W TH F S	

ADD ALL COLUMNS FOR
DAILY TOTAL:

/ - / WEEK END TOTALS

SUN.	
MON.	
TUES.	
WED.	
THURS.	
FRI.	
SAT.	
WEEK TOTAL:	

HOW MUCH DID YOU SAVE THIS WEEK?

IS THERE EXTRA TO INVEST?

LIST YOUR WEEK TOTAL AND MONEY SAVED ON THE MONTHLY BUDGET TRACKER.

THINK OF WAYS TO CUT BACK ON UNNECESSARY SPENDING, OR HOW TO SPEND MORE EFFICIENTLY.

Wealth Budget Planner

Monthly Budget Tracker

Subtract your week end totals from your discretionary income	
Discretionary Income	
Week 1.	
Week 2.	
Week 3.	
Week 4.	
Week 5.	
Surplus Cash:	

Savings
Add savings 1-5 for total savings
1.
2.
3.
4.
5.
Total Savings:

"Wealth is a tool of freedom but the pursuit of wealth is the way to slavery."

Frank Herbert

Budget Check

Are you spending more or less than planned for the month?

Are you happy with your surplus amount of cash?

Did you meet your savings goal for the month?

Are there expenses that could be reduced or eliminated, by a change in behavior?

Did you generate any extra income?

Think of some things you can do to increase your surplus cash and write them down.

Every month you should learn something new or perfect an existing skill, research assets to acquire, invest in stocks, and focus on creating income streams. Create a habit of success. Strike through all that apply during this month.

Researched Assets	Read a book	Perfected a skill
Invested in stocks	Thought of new income streams	Set new goals
Learned a new Skill	Wrote Down Ideas	Relaxed

....

....

....

If missed anything you wanted to do, be honest and write down what stopped you. Try your best to remove or change obstacles that stifle your success.

....

....

....

....

Financial Strategies & Calculations

Savings Goals, Cutbacks, Investing, Formulas, & Strategies

Financial Strategies & Calculations

Savings Goals, Cutbacks, Investing, Formulas, & Strategies

MEMO 06

FEDERAL RESERVE NOTE
THE UNITED STATES OF AMERICA
THIS NOTE IS LEGAL TENDER FOR ALL DEBTS, PUBLIC AND PRIVATE
L 89823401 J
WASHINGTON, D.C.
12
L
L 89823401 J
ONE DOLLAR

Wealth Budget Planner

Monthly Overview

Month: Yr:

Income	Amt.		Income	Amt.	
					Add totals A & B to calculate your total monthly income
Total A		+	Total B		=

Expense	Amt.		Expense	Amt.	
					Add totals C & D to calculate your total monthly expenses
Total C		+	Total D		=

Monthly Income - Monthly Expenses	-
Discretionary Income	

Spend less than you earn and do more with less.

$100\left(\frac{\text{Monthly Expenses}}{\text{Monthly Income}}\right)$	$100\left(\frac{\qquad}{\qquad}\right)$
Debt To Income Ratio %	

Increase your discretionary income by reducing expenses, or generating more income. It is key to saving, investing, and being financially free.

Aim for a debt to income ratio of less <36%. This ratio is an indicator of your default risk. The lower the better.

Wealth Budget Planner

Bill Tracker

Month: Yr:

Bill	Amt. Due	Due Date	Amt. Paid	Paid Date	Paid On Time
					Yes No
					Yes No
					Yes No
					Yes No
					Yes No
					Yes No
					Yes No
					Yes No
					Yes No
					Yes No
					Yes No
					Yes No
					Yes No
					Yes No
					Yes No
					Yes No
					Yes No
					Yes No
					Yes No
					Yes No
					Yes No
					Yes No
					Yes No
					Yes No

Wealth Budget Planner

Calendar

Month: Yr:

	Sunday	Monday	Tuesday	Wednesday	Thursday	Friday	Saturday
Save Invest Build							
Dream Plan Live							
Save Invest Build							
Dream Plan Live							
Save Invest Build							

NOTES & REMINDERS

SPECIAL OCCASIONS, ITEMS TO BUY, APPOINTMENTS, & TO DO LISTS

Weekly Spending Tracker

Wk.#

/ / S M T W TH F S	
Add all columns for Daily Total:	

/ / S M T W TH F S	
Add all columns for Daily Total:	

/ / S M T W TH F S	
Add all columns for Daily Total:	

/ / S M T W TH F S	
Add all columns for Daily Total:	

Wealth Budget Planner

Weekly Spending Tracker

Wk.#

/ / S M T W TH F S	

Add all columns for
Daily Total:

/ / S M T W TH F S	

Add all columns for
Daily Total:

/ / S M T W TH F S	

Add all columns for
Daily Total:

/ - / Week End Totals

Sun.	
Mon.	
Tues.	
Wed.	
Thurs.	
Fri.	
Sat.	
Week Total:	

How much did you save this week?

Is there extra to invest?

List your week total and money saved on the monthly budget tracker.

Think of ways to cut back on unnecessary spending, or how to spend more efficiently.

Wealth Budget Planner

Weekly Spending Tracker

Wk.#

/ / S M T W TH F S	
Add all columns for Daily Total:	

/ / S M T W TH F S	
Add all columns for Daily Total:	

/ / S M T W TH F S	
Add all columns for Daily Total:	

/ / S M T W TH F S	
Add all columns for Daily Total:	

Wealth Budget Planner

Weekly Spending Tracker

Wk.#

/ / S M T W TH F S	
Add all columns for Daily Total:	

/ / S M T W TH F S	
Add all columns for Daily Total:	

/ / S M T W TH F S	
Add all columns for Daily Total:	

/ - /	Week End Totals
Sun.	
Mon.	
Tues.	
Wed.	
Thurs.	
Fri.	
Sat.	
Week Total:	

How much did you save this week?

Is there extra to invest?

List your week total and money saved on the monthly budget tracker.

Think of ways to cut back on unnecessary spending, or how to spend more efficiently.

WEALTH BUDGET PLANNER

WEEKLY SPENDING TRACKER

WK.#

/ / S M T W TH F S	

ADD ALL COLUMNS FOR
DAILY TOTAL:

/ / S M T W TH F S	

ADD ALL COLUMNS FOR
DAILY TOTAL:

/ / S M T W TH F S	

ADD ALL COLUMNS FOR
DAILY TOTAL:

/ / S M T W TH F S	

ADD ALL COLUMNS FOR
DAILY TOTAL:

WEALTH BUDGET PLANNER

WEEKLY SPENDING TRACKER

WK.#

/ / S M T W TH F S	
ADD ALL COLUMNS FOR DAILY TOTAL:	

/ / S M T W TH F S	
ADD ALL COLUMNS FOR DAILY TOTAL:	

/ / S M T W TH F S	
ADD ALL COLUMNS FOR DAILY TOTAL:	

/ - /	WEEK END TOTALS
SUN.	
MON.	
TUES.	
WED.	
THURS.	
FRI.	
SAT.	
WEEK TOTAL:	

HOW MUCH DID YOU SAVE THIS WEEK?

IS THERE EXTRA TO INVEST?

LIST YOUR WEEK TOTAL AND MONEY SAVED ON THE MONTHLY BUDGET TRACKER.

THINK OF WAYS TO CUT BACK ON UNNECESSARY SPENDING, OR HOW TO SPEND MORE EFFICIENTLY.

Wealth Budget Planner

Weekly Spending Tracker

Wk. #

/ / S M T W TH F S

Add all columns for
Daily Total:

/ / S M T W TH F S

Add all columns for
Daily Total:

/ / S M T W TH F S

Add all columns for
Daily Total:

/ / S M T W TH F S

Add all columns for
Daily Total:

Wealth Budget Planner

Weekly Spending Tracker

Wk.#

/ / S M T W TH F S	
Add all columns for Daily Total:	

/ / S M T W TH F S	
Add all columns for Daily Total:	

/ / S M T W TH F S	
Add all columns for Daily Total:	

/ - /	Week End Totals
Sun.	
Mon.	
Tues.	
Wed.	
Thurs.	
Fri.	
Sat.	
Week Total:	

How much did you save this week?

Is there extra to invest?

List your week total and money saved on the monthly budget tracker.

Think of ways to cut back on unnecessary spending, or how to spend more efficiently.

WEALTH BUDGET PLANNER

WEEKLY SPENDING TRACKER

WK.#

/ / S M T W TH F S	

ADD ALL COLUMNS FOR
DAILY TOTAL:

/ / S M T W TH F S	

ADD ALL COLUMNS FOR
DAILY TOTAL:

/ / S M T W TH F S	

ADD ALL COLUMNS FOR
DAILY TOTAL:

/ / S M T W TH F S	

ADD ALL COLUMNS FOR
DAILY TOTAL:

Wealth Budget Planner

Weekly Spending Tracker

Wk.#

/ / S M T W TH F S	
Add all columns for Daily Total:	

/ / S M T W TH F S	
Add all columns for Daily Total:	

/ / S M T W TH F S	
Add all columns for Daily Total:	

/ - /	Week End Totals
Sun.	
Mon.	
Tues.	
Wed.	
Thurs.	
Fri.	
Sat.	
Week Total:	

How much did you save this week?

Is there extra to invest?

List your week total and money saved on the monthly budget tracker.

Think of ways to cut back on unnecessary spending, or how to spend more efficiently.

Wealth Budget Planner

Monthly Budget Tracker

Subtract your week end totals from your discretionary income	
Discretionary Income	
Week 1.	
Week 2.	
Week 3.	
Week 4.	
Week 5.	
Surplus Cash:	

Savings
Add savings 1-5 for total savings
1.
2.
3.
4.
5.
Total Savings:

"He is richest who is content with the least, for content is the wealth of nature."

Socrates

Budget Check

Are you spending more or less than planned for the month?

Are you happy with your surplus amount of cash?

Did you meet your savings goal for the month?

Are there expenses that could be reduced or eliminated, by a change in behavior?

Did you generate any extra income?

Think of some things you can do to increase your surplus cash and write them down.

Every month you should learn something new or perfect an existing skill, research assets to acquire, invest in stocks, and focus on creating income streams. Create a habit of success. Strike through all that apply during this month.

Researched Assets	Read a book	Perfected a skill
Invested in stocks	Thought of new income streams	Set new goals
Learned a new skill	Wrote Down Ideas	Relaxed

If missed anything you wanted to do, be honest and write down what stopped you. Try your best to remove or change obstacles that stifle your success.

Financial Strategies & Calculations

Savings Goals, Cutbacks, Investing, Formulas, & Strategies

Financial Strategies & Calculations

Savings Goals, Cutbacks, Investing, Formulas, & Strategies

MEMO 07

Wealth Budget Planner

Monthly Overview

Month: Yr:

Income	Amt.		Income	Amt.	
					Add totals A & B to calculate your total monthly income
Total A		+	Total B		=

Expense	Amt.		Expense	Amt.	
					Add totals C & D to calculate your total monthly expenses
Total C		+	Total D		=

Monthly Income - Monthly Expenses	-	Spend less than you earn and do more with less.	$100\left(\frac{\text{Monthly Expenses}}{\text{Monthly Income}}\right)$	$100(\rule{2cm}{0.4pt})$
Discretionary Income			Debt To Income Ratio %	

Increase your discretionary income by reducing expenses, or generating more income. It is key to saving, investing, and being financially free.

Aim for a debt to income ratio of less <36%. This ratio is an indicator of your default risk. The lower the better.

Bill Tracker

Month: **Yr:**

Bill	Amt. Due	Due Date	Amt. Paid	Paid Date	Paid On Time
					Yes No
					Yes No
					Yes No
					Yes No
					Yes No
					Yes No
					Yes No
					Yes No
					Yes No
					Yes No
					Yes No
					Yes No
					Yes No
					Yes No
					Yes No
					Yes No
					Yes No
					Yes No
					Yes No
					Yes No
					Yes No
					Yes No
					Yes No
					Yes No

Wealth Budget Planner

Calendar

Month: Yr:

	Sunday	Monday	Tuesday	Wednesday	Thursday	Friday	Saturday
Save Invest Build							
Dream Plan Live							
Save Invest Build							
Dream Plan Live							
Save Invest Build							

Notes & Reminders

Special occasions, Items to buy, Appointments, & To Do Lists

Wealth Budget Planner

Weekly Spending Tracker

Wk.#

/ / S M T W TH F S

Add all columns for
Daily Total:

/ / S M T W TH F S

Add all columns for
Daily Total:

/ / S M T W TH F S

Add all columns for
Daily Total:

/ / S M T W TH F S

Add all columns for
Daily Total:

Wealth Budget Planner

Weekly Spending Tracker

Wk.#

/ / S M T W TH F S	
Add all columns for Daily Total:	

/ / S M T W TH F S	
Add all columns for Daily Total:	

/ / S M T W TH F S	
Add all columns for Daily Total:	

/ - /	Week End Totals
Sun.	
Mon.	
Tues.	
Wed.	
Thurs.	
Fri.	
Sat.	
Week Total:	

How much did you save this week?

Is there extra to invest?

List your week total and money saved on the monthly budget tracker.

Think of ways to cut back on unnecessary spending, or how to spend more efficiently.

Wealth Budget Planner

Weekly Spending Tracker

Wk.#

/ / S M T W TH F S

Add all columns for
Daily Total:

/ / S M T W TH F S

Add all columns for
Daily Total:

/ / S M T W TH F S

Add all columns for
Daily Total:

/ / S M T W TH F S

Add all columns for
Daily Total:

Wealth Budget Planner

Weekly Spending Tracker

Wk.#

/ / S M T W TH F S	
Add all columns for Daily Total:	

/ / S M T W TH F S	
Add all columns for Daily Total:	

/ / S M T W TH F S	
Add all columns for Daily Total:	

/ - / Week End Totals

Sun.	
Mon.	
Tues.	
Wed.	
Thurs.	
Fri.	
Sat.	
Week Total:	

How much did you save this week?

Is there extra to invest?

List your week total and money saved on the monthly budget tracker.

Think of ways to cut back on unnecessary spending, or how to spend more efficiently.

Wealth Budget Planner

Weekly Spending Tracker

Wk.#

/ / S M T W TH F S	

Add all columns for
Daily Total:

/ / S M T W TH F S	

Add all columns for
Daily Total:

/ / S M T W TH F S	

Add all columns for
Daily Total:

/ / S M T W TH F S	

Add all columns for
Daily Total:

Wealth Budget Planner

Weekly Spending Tracker

Wk.#

/ / S M T W TH F S	
Add all columns for Daily Total:	

/ / S M T W TH F S	
Add all columns for Daily Total:	

/ / S M T W TH F S	
Add all columns for Daily Total:	

/ - /	Week End Totals
Sun.	
Mon.	
Tues.	
Wed.	
Thurs.	
Fri.	
Sat.	
Week Total:	

How much did you save this week?

Is there extra to invest?

List your week total and money saved on the monthly budget tracker.

Think of ways to cut back on unnecessary spending, or how to spend more efficiently.

Wealth Budget Planner

Weekly Spending Tracker

Wk.#

/ / S M T W TH F S

Add all columns for
Daily Total:

/ / S M T W TH F S

Add all columns for
Daily Total:

/ / S M T W TH F S

Add all columns for
Daily Total:

/ / S M T W TH F S

Add all columns for
Daily Total:

Wealth Budget Planner

Weekly Spending Tracker

Wk.#

/ / S M T W TH F S	
Add all columns for Daily Total:	

/ / S M T W TH F S	
Add all columns for Daily Total:	

/ / S M T W TH F S	
Add all columns for Daily Total:	

/ - / Week End Totals		
Sun.		How much did you save this week? ----------------------
Mon.		
Tues.		
Wed.		Is there extra to invest?
Thurs.		
Fri.		List your week total and money saved on the monthly budget tracker.
Sat.		
Week Total:		

Think of ways to cut back on unnecessary spending, or how to spend more efficiently.

Wealth Budget Planner

Weekly Spending Tracker

Wk.#

/ / S M T W TH F S

Add all columns for
Daily Total:

/ / S M T W TH F S

Add all columns for
Daily Total:

/ / S M T W TH F S

Add all columns for
Daily Total:

/ / S M T W TH F S

Add all columns for
Daily Total:

Wealth Budget Planner

Weekly Spending Tracker

Wk.#

/ / S M T W TH F S	
Add all columns for Daily Total:	

/ / S M T W TH F S	
Add all columns for Daily Total:	

/ / S M T W TH F S	
Add all columns for Daily Total:	

/ - / Week End Totals

Sun.	
Mon.	
Tues.	
Wed.	
Thurs.	
Fri.	
Sat.	
Week Total:	

How much did you save this week?

Is there extra to invest?

List your week total and money saved on the monthly budget tracker.

Think of ways to cut back on unnecessary spending, or how to spend more efficiently.

Wealth Budget Planner

Monthly Budget Tracker

Subtract your week end totals from your discretionary income		Savings
Discretionary Income		Add savings 1-5 for total savings
Week 1.		1.
Week 2.		2.
Week 3.		3.
Week 4.		4.
Week 5.		5.
Surplus Cash:		Total Savings:

"Never develop a habit of buying things you don't need, with money you don't have."

Jay Porter

Budget Check

Are you spending more or less than planned for the month?

Are you happy with your surplus amount of cash?

Did you meet your savings goal for the month?

Are there expenses that could be reduced or eliminated, by a change in behavior?

Did you generate any extra income?

Think of some things you can do to increase your surplus cash and write them down.

Every month you should learn something new or perfect an existing skill, research assets to acquire, invest in stocks, and focus on creating income streams. Create a habit of success. Strike through all that apply during this month.

Researched Assets	Read a book	Perfected a skill
Invested in stocks	Thought of new income streams	Set new goals
Learned a new Skill	Wrote Down Ideas	Relaxed

If missed anything you wanted to do, be honest and write down what stopped you. Try your best to remove or change obstacles that stifle your success.

Financial Strategies & Calculations

Savings Goals, Cutbacks, Investing, Formulas, & Strategies

Financial Strategies & Calculations

Savings Goals, Cutbacks, Investing, Formulas, & Strategies

MEMO
08

enter
return
shift
THURS
FRI
SAT
SUN
MON
TUE
WED
THUR
DAY OFF
BRAM
DAY OFF
4-6pm

Wealth Budget Planner

Monthly Overview

Month: Yr:

Income	Amt.		Income	Amt.	
					Add totals A & B to calculate your total monthly income
Total A		+	Total B		=

Expense	Amt.		Expense	Amt.	
					Add totals C & D to calculate your total monthly expenses
Total C		+	Total D		=

Monthly Income - Monthly Expenses	-	Spend less than you earn and do more with less.	$100\left(\frac{\text{Expenses}}{\text{Monthly Income}}\right)$ Monthly	$100\left(\frac{\quad}{\quad}\right)$
Discretionary Income			Debt To Income Ratio %	

Increase your discretionary income by reducing expenses, or generating more income. It is key to saving, investing, and being financially free.

Aim for a debt to income ratio of less <36%. This ratio is an indicator of your default risk. The lower the better.

Wealth Budget Planner

Bill Tracker

Month: Yr:

Bill	Amt. Due	Due Date	Amt. Paid	Paid Date	Paid On Time
					Yes No
					Yes No
					Yes No
					Yes No
					Yes No
					Yes No
					Yes No
					Yes No
					Yes No
					Yes No
					Yes No
					Yes No
					Yes No
					Yes No
					Yes No
					Yes No
					Yes No
					Yes No
					Yes No
					Yes No
					Yes No
					Yes No
					Yes No
					Yes No

WEALTH BUDGET PLANNER

CALENDAR

MONTH: YR:

	SUNDAY	MONDAY	TUESDAY	WEDNESDAY	THURSDAY	FRIDAY	SATURDAY
SAVE INVEST BUILD							
DREAM PLAN LIVE							
SAVE INVEST BUILD							
DREAM PLAN LIVE							
SAVE INVEST BUILD							

Notes & Reminders

Special occasions, Items to buy, Appointments, & To Do Lists

Wealth Budget Planner

Weekly Spending Tracker

Wk.#

/ / S M T W TH F S	
Add all columns for Daily Total:	

/ / S M T W TH F S	
Add all columns for Daily Total:	

/ / S M T W TH F S	
Add all columns for Daily Total:	

/ / S M T W TH F S	
Add all columns for Daily Total:	

Wealth Budget Planner

Weekly Spending Tracker

Wk.#

/ / S M T W TH F S	
Add all columns for Daily Total:	

/ / S M T W TH F S	
Add all columns for Daily Total:	

/ / S M T W TH F S	
Add all columns for Daily Total:	

/ - / Week End Totals

Sun.	
Mon.	
Tues.	
Wed.	
Thurs.	
Fri.	
Sat.	
Week Total:	

How much did you save this week?

Is there extra to invest?

List your week total and money saved on the monthly budget tracker.

Think of ways to cut back on unnecessary spending, or how to spend more efficiently.

Wealth Budget Planner

Weekly Spending Tracker

Wk.#

/ / S M T W TH F S	
Add all columns for Daily Total:	

/ / S M T W TH F S	
Add all columns for Daily Total:	

/ / S M T W TH F S	
Add all columns for Daily Total:	

/ / S M T W TH F S	
Add all columns for Daily Total:	

Wealth Budget Planner

Weekly Spending Tracker

Wk.#

/ /	S M T W TH F S
Add all columns for Daily Total:	

/ /	S M T W TH F S
Add all columns for Daily Total:	

/ /	S M T W TH F S
Add all columns for Daily Total:	

/ - /	Week End Totals
Sun.	
Mon.	
Tues.	
Wed.	
Thurs.	
Fri.	
Sat.	
Week Total:	

How much did you save this week?

Is there extra to invest?

List your week total and money saved on the monthly budget tracker.

Think of ways to cut back on unnecessary spending, or how to spend more efficiently.

Wealth Budget Planner

Weekly Spending Tracker

Wk.#

/ / S M T W TH F S	
Add all columns for Daily Total:	

/ / S M T W TH F S	
Add all columns for Daily Total:	

/ / S M T W TH F S	
Add all columns for Daily Total:	

/ / S M T W TH F S	
Add all columns for Daily Total:	

Wealth Budget Planner

Weekly Spending Tracker

Wk.#

/ / S M T W TH F S	
Add all columns for Daily Total:	

/ / S M T W TH F S	
Add all columns for Daily Total:	

/ / S M T W TH F S	
Add all columns for Daily Total:	

/ - /	Week End Totals
Sun.	
Mon.	
Tues.	
Wed.	
Thurs.	
Fri.	
Sat.	
Week Total:	

How much did you save this week?

Is there extra to invest?

List your week total and money saved on the monthly budget tracker.

Think of ways to cut back on unnecessary spending, or how to spend more efficiently.

Wealth Budget Planner

Weekly Spending Tracker

Wk.#

/ / S M T W TH F S	
Add all columns for Daily Total:	

/ / S M T W TH F S	
Add all columns for Daily Total:	

/ / S M T W TH F S	
Add all columns for Daily Total:	

/ / S M T W TH F S	
Add all columns for Daily Total:	

WEALTH BUDGET PLANNER

WEEKLY SPENDING TRACKER

WK.#

/ / S M T W TH F S	
ADD ALL COLUMNS FOR DAILY TOTAL:	

/ / S M T W TH F S	
ADD ALL COLUMNS FOR DAILY TOTAL:	

/ / S M T W TH F S	
ADD ALL COLUMNS FOR DAILY TOTAL:	

/ - /	WEEK END TOTALS
SUN.	
MON.	
TUES.	
WED.	
THURS.	
FRI.	
SAT.	
WEEK TOTAL:	

HOW MUCH DID YOU SAVE THIS WEEK?

IS THERE EXTRA TO INVEST?

LIST YOUR WEEK TOTAL AND MONEY SAVED ON THE MONTHLY BUDGET TRACKER.

THINK OF WAYS TO CUT BACK ON UNNECESSARY SPENDING, OR HOW TO SPEND MORE EFFICIENTLY.

WEALTH BUDGET PLANNER

WEEKLY SPENDING TRACKER

WK.#

/ / S M T W TH F S	

ADD ALL COLUMNS FOR
DAILY TOTAL:

/ / S M T W TH F S	

ADD ALL COLUMNS FOR
DAILY TOTAL:

/ / S M T W TH F S	

ADD ALL COLUMNS FOR
DAILY TOTAL:

/ / S M T W TH F S	

ADD ALL COLUMNS FOR
DAILY TOTAL:

Wealth Budget Planner

Weekly Spending Tracker

Wk.#

/ / S M T W TH F S	
Add all columns for Daily Total:	

/ / S M T W TH F S	
Add all columns for Daily Total:	

/ / S M T W TH F S	
Add all columns for Daily Total:	

/ - / Week End Totals

Sun.	
Mon.	
Tues.	
Wed.	
Thurs.	
Fri.	
Sat.	
Week Total:	

How much did you save this week?

Is there extra to invest?

List your week total and money saved on the monthly budget tracker.

Think of ways to cut back on unnecessary spending, or how to spend more efficiently.

Wealth Budget Planner

Monthly Budget Tracker

Subtract your week end totals from your discretionary income	
Discretionary Income	
Week 1.	
Week 2.	
Week 3.	
Week 4.	
Week 5.	
Surplus Cash:	

Savings
Add savings 1-5 for total savings
1.
2.
3.
4.
5.
Total Savings:

"Nothing ever comes to one, that is worth having, except as a result of hard work."

Booker T. Washington

Budget Check

Are you spending more or less than planned for the month?

Are you happy with your surplus amount of cash?

Did you meet your savings goal for the month?

Are there expenses that could be reduced or eliminated, by a change in behavior?

Did you generate any extra income?

Think of some things you can do to increase your surplus cash and write them down.

Every month you should learn something new or perfect an existing skill, research assets to acquire, invest in stocks, and focus on creating income streams. Create a habit of success. Strike through all that apply during this month.

Researched Assets	Read a book	Perfected a skill
Invested in stocks	Thought of new income streams	Set new goals
Learned a new Skill	Wrote Down Ideas	Relaxed

If missed anything you wanted to do, be honest and write down what stopped you. Try your best to remove or change obstacles that stifle your success.

FINANCIAL STRATEGIES & CALCULATIONS

SAVINGS GOALS, CUTBACKS, INVESTING, FORMULAS, & STRATEGIES

Wealth Budget Planner

Financial Strategies & Calculations

Savings Goals, Cutbacks, Investing, Formulas, & Strategies

MEMO 09

Wealth Budget Planner

Monthly Overview

Month: Yr:

Income	Amt.		Income	Amt.	
					Add totals A & B to calculate your total monthly income
Total A		+	Total B		=

Expense	Amt.		Expense	Amt.	
					Add totals C & D to calculate your total monthly expenses
Total C		+	Total D		=

Monthly Income - Monthly Expenses	-	Spend less than you earn and do more with less.	$100\left(\frac{\text{Expenses}}{\text{Monthly Income}}\right)$	$100\left(\frac{\quad}{\quad}\right)$
Discretionary Income			Debt To Income Ratio %	

Increase your discretionary income by reducing expenses, or generating more income. It is key to saving, investing, and being financially free.

Aim for a debt to income ratio of less <36%. This ratio is an indicator of your default risk. The lower the better.

BILL TRACKER

MONTH: YR:

BILL	AMT. DUE	DUE DATE	AMT. PAID	PAID DATE	PAID ON TIME
					YES NO
					YES NO
					YES NO
					YES NO
					YES NO
					YES NO
					YES NO
					YES NO
					YES NO
					YES NO
					YES NO
					YES NO
					YES NO
					YES NO
					YES NO
					YES NO
					YES NO
					YES NO
					YES NO
					YES NO
					YES NO
					YES NO
					YES NO
					YES NO

Wealth Budget Planner

Calendar

Month:

Yr:

	Sunday	Monday	Tuesday	Wednesday	Thursday	Friday	Saturday
Save Invest Build							
Dream Plan Live							
Save Invest Build							
Dream Plan Live							
Save Invest Build							

NOTES & REMINDERS

SPECIAL OCCASIONS, ITEMS TO BUY, APPOINTMENTS, & TO DO LISTS

WEALTH BUDGET PLANNER

WEEKLY SPENDING TRACKER

WK.#

/ / S M T W TH F S	
ADD ALL COLUMNS FOR DAILY TOTAL:	

/ / S M T W TH F S	
ADD ALL COLUMNS FOR DAILY TOTAL:	

/ / S M T W TH F S	
ADD ALL COLUMNS FOR DAILY TOTAL:	

/ / S M T W TH F S	
ADD ALL COLUMNS FOR DAILY TOTAL:	

Wealth Budget Planner

Weekly Spending Tracker

Wk.#

/ / S M T W TH F S	
Add all columns for Daily Total:	

/ / S M T W TH F S	
Add all columns for Daily Total:	

/ / S M T W TH F S	
Add all columns for Daily Total:	

/ - / Week End Totals

Sun.	
Mon.	
Tues.	
Wed.	
Thurs.	
Fri.	
Sat.	
Week Total:	

How much did you save this week?

Is there extra to invest?

List your week total and money saved on the monthly budget tracker.

Think of ways to cut back on unnecessary spending, or how to spend more efficiently.

Wealth Budget Planner

Weekly Spending Tracker

Wk.#

/ / S M T W TH F S

Add all columns for
Daily Total:

/ / S M T W TH F S

Add all columns for
Daily Total:

/ / S M T W TH F S

Add all columns for
Daily Total:

/ / S M T W TH F S

Add all columns for
Daily Total:

Wealth Budget Planner

Weekly Spending Tracker

Wk.#

/ / S M T W TH F S	
Add all columns for Daily Total:	

/ / S M T W TH F S	
Add all columns for Daily Total:	

/ / S M T W TH F S	
Add all columns for Daily Total:	

/ - / Week End Totals

Sun.	
Mon.	
Tues.	
Wed.	
Thurs.	
Fri.	
Sat.	
Week Total:	

How much did you save this week?

Is there extra to invest?

List your week total and money saved on the monthly budget tracker.

Think of ways to cut back on unnecessary spending, or how to spend more efficiently.

Wealth Budget Planner

Weekly Spending Tracker

Wk.#

/ / S M T W TH F S	
Add all columns for Daily Total:	

/ / S M T W TH F S	
Add all columns for Daily Total:	

/ / S M T W TH F S	
Add all columns for Daily Total:	

/ / S M T W TH F S	
Add all columns for Daily Total:	

Wealth Budget Planner

Weekly Spending Tracker

Wk.#

/ / S M T W TH F S	
Add all columns for Daily Total:	

/ / S M T W TH F S	
Add all columns for Daily Total:	

/ / S M T W TH F S	
Add all columns for Daily Total:	

/ - /	Week End Totals
Sun.	
Mon.	
Tues.	
Wed.	
Thurs.	
Fri.	
Sat.	
Week Total:	

How much did you save this week?

Is there extra to invest?

List your week total and money saved on the monthly budget tracker.

Think of ways to cut back on unnecessary spending, or how to spend more efficiently.

Weekly Spending Tracker

Wk.#

/ / S M T W TH F S	
Add all columns for Daily Total:	

/ / S M T W TH F S	
Add all columns for Daily Total:	

/ / S M T W TH F S	
Add all columns for Daily Total:	

/ / S M T W TH F S	
Add all columns for Daily Total:	

WEALTH BUDGET PLANNER

WEEKLY SPENDING TRACKER

WK.#

/ / S M T W TH F S	
ADD ALL COLUMNS FOR DAILY TOTAL:	

/ / S M T W TH F S	
ADD ALL COLUMNS FOR DAILY TOTAL:	

/ / S M T W TH F S	
ADD ALL COLUMNS FOR DAILY TOTAL:	

/ - /	WEEK END TOTALS
SUN.	
MON.	
TUES.	
WED.	
THURS.	
FRI.	
SAT.	
WEEK TOTAL:	

HOW MUCH DID YOU SAVE THIS WEEK?

IS THERE EXTRA TO INVEST?

LIST YOUR WEEK TOTAL AND MONEY SAVED ON THE MONTHLY BUDGET TRACKER.

THINK OF WAYS TO CUT BACK ON UNNECESSARY SPENDING, OR HOW TO SPEND MORE EFFICIENTLY.

Wealth Budget Planner

Weekly Spending Tracker

Wk.#

/ / S M T W TH F S	
Add all columns for Daily Total:	

/ / S M T W TH F S	
Add all columns for Daily Total:	

/ / S M T W TH F S	
Add all columns for Daily Total:	

/ / S M T W TH F S	
Add all columns for Daily Total:	

Wealth Budget Planner

Weekly Spending Tracker

Wk.#

/ / S M T W TH F S	

Add all columns for
Daily Total:

/ / S M T W TH F S	

Add all columns for
Daily Total:

/ / S M T W TH F S	

Add all columns for
Daily Total:

/ - / Week End Totals

Sun.	
Mon.	
Tues.	
Wed.	
Thurs.	
Fri.	
Sat.	
Week Total:	

How much did you save this week?

Is there extra to invest?

List your week total and money saved on the monthly budget tracker.

Think of ways to cut back on unnecessary spending, or how to spend more efficiently.

Wealth Budget Planner

Monthly Budget Tracker

Subtract your week end totals from your discretionary income	
Discretionary Income	
Week 1.	
Week 2.	
Week 3.	
Week 4.	
Week 5.	
Surplus Cash:	

Savings
Add savings 1-5 for total savings
1.
2.
3.
4.
5.
Total Savings:

"Im a cash flow guy. If it doesn't make me money today, forget about it."

Robert Kiyosaki

Budget Check

Are you spending more or less than planned for the month?

Are you happy with your surplus amount of cash?

Did you meet your savings goal for the month?

Are there expenses that could be reduced or eliminated, by a change in behavior?

Did you generate any extra income?

Think of some things you can do to increase your surplus cash and write them down.

Every month you should learn something new or perfect an existing skill, research assets to acquire, invest in stocks, and focus on creating income streams. Create a habit of success. Strike through all that apply during this month.

Researched Assets	Read a book	Perfected a skill
Invested in stocks	Thought of new income streams	Set new goals
Learned a new Skill	Wrote Down Ideas	Relaxed

If missed anything you wanted to do, be honest and write down what stopped you. Try your best to remove or change obstacles that stifle your success.

Financial Strategies & Calculations

Savings Goals, Cutbacks, Investing, Formulas, & Strategies

Financial Strategies & Calculations

Savings Goals, Cutbacks, Investing, Formulas, & Strategies

MEMO 10

Wealth Budget Planner

Monthly Overview

Month: Yr:

Income	Amt.		Income	Amt.	
					Add totals A & B to calculate your total monthly income
Total A		+	Total B		=

Expense	Amt.		Expense	Amt.	
					Add totals C & D to calculate your total monthly expenses
Total C		+	Total D		=

Monthly Income - Monthly Expenses	-	Spend less than you earn and do more with less.	$100\left(\frac{\text{Expenses}}{\text{Monthly Income}}\right)$	$100\left(\frac{}{}\right)$
Discretionary Income			Debt To Income Ratio %	

Increase your discretionary income by reducing expenses, or generating more income. It is key to saving, investing, and being financially free.

Aim for a debt to income ratio of less <36%. This ratio is an indicator of your default risk. The lower the better.

Wealth Budget Planner

Bill Tracker

Month: Yr:

Bill	Amt. Due	Due Date	Amt. Paid	Paid Date	Paid On Time
					Yes No
					Yes No
					Yes No
					Yes No
					Yes No
					Yes No
					Yes No
					Yes No
					Yes No
					Yes No
					Yes No
					Yes No
					Yes No
					Yes No
					Yes No
					Yes Time
					Yes No
					Yes No
					Yes No
					Yes No
					Yes No
					Yes No
					Yes No
					Yes No

Wealth Budget Planner

Calendar

Month: Yr:

	Sunday	Monday	Tuesday	Wednesday	Thursday	Friday	Saturday
Save Invest Build							
Dream Plan Live							
Save Invest Build							
Dream Plan Live							
Save Invest Build							

Notes & Reminders

Special occasions, Items to buy, Appointments, & To Do Lists

Wealth Budget Planner

Weekly Spending Tracker

Wk.#

/ / S M T W TH F S	
Add all columns for Daily Total:	

/ / S M T W TH F S	
Add all columns for Daily Total:	

/ / S M T W TH F S	
Add all columns for Daily Total:	

/ / S M T W TH F S	
Add all columns for Daily Total:	

Wealth Budget Planner

Weekly Spending Tracker

Wk.#

/ /	S M T W TH F S
Add all columns for Daily Total:	

/ /	S M T W TH F S
Add all columns for Daily Total:	

/ /	S M T W TH F S
Add all columns for Daily Total:	

/ - / Week End Totals

Sun.	
Mon.	
Tues.	
Wed.	
Thurs.	
Fri.	
Sat.	
Week Total:	

How much did you save this week?

Is there extra to invest?

List your week total and money saved on the monthly budget tracker.

Think of ways to cut back on unnecessary spending, or how to spend more efficiently.

Wealth Budget Planner

Weekly Spending Tracker

Wk.#

/ / S M T W TH F S

ADD ALL COLUMNS FOR
DAILY TOTAL:

/ / S M T W TH F S

ADD ALL COLUMNS FOR
DAILY TOTAL:

/ / S M T W TH F S

ADD ALL COLUMNS FOR
DAILY TOTAL:

/ / S M T W TH F S

ADD ALL COLUMNS FOR
DAILY TOTAL:

Wealth Budget Planner

Weekly Spending Tracker

Wk.#

/ / S M T W TH F S

Add all columns for
Daily Total:

/ / S M T W TH F S

Add all columns for
Daily Total:

/ / S M T W TH F S

Add all columns for
Daily Total:

/ - / Week End Totals

Sun.	
Mon.	
Tues.	
Wed.	
Thurs.	
Fri.	
Sat.	
Week Total:	

How much did you save this week?

Is there extra to invest?

List your week total and money saved on the monthly budget tracker.

Think of ways to cut back on unnecessary spending, or how to spend more efficiently.

Wealth Budget Planner

Weekly Spending Tracker

Wk.#

/ / S M T W TH F S	
Add all columns for Daily Total:	

/ / S M T W TH F S	
Add all columns for Daily Total:	

/ / S M T W TH F S	
Add all columns for Daily Total:	

/ / S M T W TH F S	
Add all columns for Daily Total:	

Wealth Budget Planner

Weekly Spending Tracker

Wk.#

/ /	S M T W TH F S
Add all columns for Daily Total:	

/ /	S M T W TH F S
Add all columns for Daily Total:	

/ /	S M T W TH F S
Add all columns for Daily Total:	

/ - / Week End Totals

Sun.	
Mon.	
Tues.	
Wed.	
Thurs.	
Fri.	
Sat.	
Week Total:	

How much did you save this week?

Is there extra to invest?

List your week total and money saved on the monthly budget tracker.

Think of ways to cut back on unnecessary spending, or how to spend more efficiently.

Wealth Budget Planner

Weekly Spending Tracker

Wk.#

/ / S M T W TH F S	
Add all columns for Daily Total:	

/ / S M T W TH F S	
Add all columns for Daily Total:	

/ / S M T W TH F S	
Add all columns for Daily Total:	

/ / S M T W TH F S	
Add all columns for Daily Total:	

Wealth Budget Planner

Weekly Spending Tracker

Wk.#

/ / S M T W TH F S	
Add all columns for Daily Total:	

/ / S M T W TH F S	
Add all columns for Daily Total:	

/ / S M T W TH F S	
Add all columns for Daily Total:	

/ - /	Week End Totals
Sun.	
Mon.	
Tues.	
Wed.	
Thurs.	
Fri.	
Sat.	
Week Total:	

How much did you save this week?

Is there extra to invest?

List your week total and money saved on the monthly budget tracker.

Think of ways to cut back on unnecessary spending, or how to spend more efficiently.

WEALTH BUDGET PLANNER

WEEKLY SPENDING TRACKER

WK.#

/ / S M T W TH F S	
ADD ALL COLUMNS FOR DAILY TOTAL:	

/ / S M T W TH F S	
ADD ALL COLUMNS FOR DAILY TOTAL:	

/ / S M T W TH F S	
ADD ALL COLUMNS FOR DAILY TOTAL:	

/ / S M T W TH F S	
ADD ALL COLUMNS FOR DAILY TOTAL:	

Wealth Budget Planner

Weekly Spending Tracker

Wk.#

/ /	S M T W TH F S
Add all columns for **Daily Total:**	

/ /	S M T W TH F S
Add all columns for **Daily Total:**	

/ /	S M T W TH F S
Add all columns for **Daily Total:**	

/ - /	Week End Totals
Sun.	
Mon.	
Tues.	
Wed.	
Thurs.	
Fri.	
Sat.	
Week Total:	

How much did you save this week?

Is there extra to invest?

List your week total and money saved on the monthly budget tracker.

Think of ways to cut back on unnecessary spending, or how to spend more efficiently.

Wealth Budget Planner

Monthly Budget Tracker

Subtract your week end totals from your discretionary income	
Discretionary Income	
Week 1.	
Week 2.	
Week 3.	
Week 4.	
Week 5.	
Surplus Cash:	

Savings
Add savings 1-5 for total savings
1.
2.
3.
4.
5.
Total Savings:

"Treat every dollar as an employee that needs to be gainfully employed."

Jay Porter

Budget Check

Are you spending more or less than planned for the month?

Are you happy with your surplus amount of cash?

Did you meet your savings goal for the month?

Are there expenses that could be reduced or eliminated, by a change in behavior?

Did you generate any extra income?

Think of some things you can do to increase your surplus cash and write them down.

Every month you should learn something new or perfect an existing skill, research assets to acquire, invest in stocks, and focus on creating income streams. Create a habit of success. Strike through all that apply during this month.

Researched Assets	Read a book	Perfected a skill
Invested in stocks	Thought of new income streams	Set new goals
Learned a new Skill	Wrote Down Ideas	Relaxed

If missed anything you wanted to do, be honest and write down what stopped you. Try your best to remove or change obstacles that stifle your success.

Financial Strategies & Calculations

Savings Goals, Cutbacks, Investing, Formulas, & Strategies

FINANCIAL STRATEGIES & CALCULATIONS

SAVINGS GOALS, CUTBACKS, INVESTING, FORMULAS, & STRATEGIES

MEMO 11

Wealth Budget Planner

Monthly Overview

Month: Yr:

Income	Amt.		Income	Amt.	
					Add totals A & B to calculate your total monthly income
Total A		+	Total B		=

Expense	Amt.		Expense	Amt.	
					Add totals C & D to calculate your total monthly expenses
Total C		+	Total D		=

Monthly Income - Monthly Expenses	-	Spend less than you earn and do more with less.	$100\left(\frac{\text{Monthly Expenses}}{\text{Monthly Income}}\right)$	$100\left(\frac{\quad}{\quad}\right)$
Discretionary Income			Debt To Income Ratio %	

Increase your discretionary income by reducing expenses, or generating more income. It is key to saving, investing, and being financially free.

Aim for a debt to income ratio of less <36%. This ratio is an indicator of your default risk. The lower the better.

Wealth Budget Planner

Bill Tracker

Month: Yr:

Bill	Amt. Due	Due Date	Amt. Paid	Paid Date	Paid On Time
					Yes No
					Yes No
					Yes No
					Yes No
					Yes No
					Yes No
					Yes No
					Yes No
					Yes No
					Yes No
					Yes No
					Yes No
					Yes No
					Yes No
					Yes No
					Yes No
					Yes No
					Yes No
					Yes No
					Yes No
					Yes No
					Yes No
					Yes No
					Yes No

Wealth Budget Planner

Calendar

Month: Yr:

	Sunday	Monday	Tuesday	Wednesday	Thursday	Friday	Saturday
Save Invest Build							
Dream Plan Live							
Save Invest Build							
Dream Plan Live							
Save Invest Build							

NOTES & REMINDERS

SPECIAL OCCASIONS, ITEMS TO BUY, APPOINTMENTS, & TO DO LISTS

Wealth Budget Planner

Weekly Spending Tracker

Wk.#

/ / S M T W TH F S	
Add all columns for Daily Total:	

/ / S M T W TH F S	
Add all columns for Daily Total:	

/ / S M T W TH F S	
Add all columns for Daily Total:	

/ / S M T W TH F S	
Add all columns for Daily Total:	

Wealth Budget Planner

Weekly Spending Tracker

Wk.#

/ / S M T W TH F S	
Add all columns for Daily Total:	

/ / S M T W TH F S	
Add all columns for Daily Total:	

/ / S M T W TH F S	
Add all columns for Daily Total:	

/ - / Week End Totals

Sun.	
Mon.	
Tues.	
Wed.	
Thurs.	
Fri.	
Sat.	
Week Total:	

How much did you save this week?

Is there extra to invest?

List your week total and money saved on the monthly budget tracker.

Think of ways to cut back on unnecessary spending, or how to spend more efficiently.

Wealth Budget Planner

Weekly Spending Tracker

Wk.#

/ / S M T W TH F S	

Add all columns for
Daily Total:

/ / S M T W TH F S	

Add all columns for
Daily Total:

/ / S M T W TH F S	

Add all columns for
Daily Total:

/ / S M T W TH F S	

Add all columns for
Daily Total:

Wealth Budget Planner

Weekly Spending Tracker

Wk.#

/ / S M T W TH F S	

Add all columns for
Daily Total:

/ / S M T W TH F S	

Add all columns for
Daily Total:

/ / S M T W TH F S	

Add all columns for
Daily Total:

/ - / Week End Totals

Sun.	
Mon.	
Tues.	
Wed.	
Thurs.	
Fri.	
Sat.	
Week Total:	

How much did you save this week?

Is there extra to invest?

List your week total and money saved on the monthly budget tracker.

Think of ways to cut back on unnecessary spending, or how to spend more efficiently.

---Wealth Budget Planner---

Weekly Spending Tracker

Wk.#

/ / S M T W TH F S	
Add all columns for Daily Total:	

/ / S M T W TH F S	
Add all columns for Daily Total:	

/ / S M T W TH F S	
Add all columns for Daily Total:	

/ / S M T W TH F S	
Add all columns for Daily Total:	

WEALTH BUDGET PLANNER

WEEKLY SPENDING TRACKER

WK.#

/ / S M T W TH F S	
ADD ALL COLUMNS FOR DAILY TOTAL:	

/ / S M T W TH F S	
ADD ALL COLUMNS FOR DAILY TOTAL:	

/ / S M T W TH F S	
ADD ALL COLUMNS FOR DAILY TOTAL:	

/ - / WEEK END TOTALS		
SUN.		HOW MUCH DID YOU SAVE THIS WEEK?
MON.		
TUES.		----------------------
WED.		IS THERE EXTRA TO INVEST?
THURS.		
FRI.		LIST YOUR WEEK TOTAL AND MONEY SAVED ON THE MONTHLY BUDGET TRACKER.
SAT.		
WEEK TOTAL:		

THINK OF WAYS TO CUT BACK ON UNNECESSARY SPENDING, OR HOW TO SPEND MORE EFFICIENTLY.

Wealth Budget Planner

Weekly Spending Tracker

Wk.#

/ / S M T W TH F S	

Add all columns for
Daily Total:

/ / S M T W TH F S	

Add all columns for
Daily Total:

/ / S M T W TH F S	

Add all columns for
Daily Total:

/ / S M T W TH F S	

Add all columns for
Daily Total:

WEALTH BUDGET PLANNER

WEEKLY SPENDING TRACKER

WK.#

/ / S M T W TH F S	
ADD ALL COLUMNS FOR DAILY TOTAL:	

/ / S M T W TH F S	
ADD ALL COLUMNS FOR DAILY TOTAL:	

/ / S M T W TH F S	
ADD ALL COLUMNS FOR DAILY TOTAL:	

/ - /	WEEK END TOTALS
SUN.	
MON.	
TUES.	
WED.	
THURS.	
FRI.	
SAT.	
WEEK TOTAL:	

HOW MUCH DID YOU SAVE THIS WEEK?

IS THERE EXTRA TO INVEST?

LIST YOUR WEEK TOTAL AND MONEY SAVED ON THE MONTHLY BUDGET TRACKER.

THINK OF WAYS TO CUT BACK ON UNNECESSARY SPENDING, OR HOW TO SPEND MORE EFFICIENTLY.

WEEKLY SPENDING TRACKER

WK.#

/ / S M T W TH F S	
ADD ALL COLUMNS FOR DAILY TOTAL:	

/ / S M T W TH F S	
ADD ALL COLUMNS FOR DAILY TOTAL:	

/ / S M T W TH F S	
ADD ALL COLUMNS FOR DAILY TOTAL:	

/ / S M T W TH F S	
ADD ALL COLUMNS FOR DAILY TOTAL:	

Wealth Budget Planner

Weekly Spending Tracker

Wk.#

/ / S M T W TH F S	

Add all columns for
Daily Total:

/ / S M T W TH F S	

Add all columns for
Daily Total:

/ / S M T W TH F S	

Add all columns for
Daily Total:

/ - / Week End Totals

Sun.	
Mon.	
Tues.	
Wed.	
Thurs.	
Fri.	
Sat.	
Week Total:	

How much did you save this week?

Is there extra to invest?

List your week total and money saved on the monthly budget tracker.

Think of ways to cut back on unnecessary spending, or how to spend more efficiently.

Wealth Budget Planner

Monthly Budget Tracker

Subtract your week end totals from your discretionary income	
Discretionary Income	
Week 1.	
Week 2.	
Week 3.	
Week 4.	
Week 5.	
Surplus Cash:	

Savings
Add savings 1-5 for total savings
1.
2.
3.
4.
5.
Total Savings:

"Wealth stays with us a little moment if at all: only our characters are steadfast not our gold." Euripides

Budget Check

Are you spending more or less than planned for the month?

Are you happy with your surplus amount of cash?

Did you meet your savings goal for the month?

Are there expenses that could be reduced or eliminated, by a change in behavior?

Did you generate any extra income?

Think of some things you can do to increase your surplus cash and write them down.

Every month you should learn something new or perfect an existing skill, research assets to acquire, invest in stocks, and focus on creating income streams. Create a habit of success. Strike through all that apply during this month.

Researched Assets	Read a book	Perfected a skill
Invested in stocks	Thought of new income streams	Set new goals
Learned a new Skill	Wrote Down Ideas	Relaxed

If missed anything you wanted to do, be honest and write down what stopped you. Try your best to remove or change obstacles that stifle your success.

Wealth Budget Planner

Financial Strategies & Calculations

Savings Goals, Cutbacks, Investing, Formulas, & Strategies

Financial Strategies & Calculations

Savings Goals, Cutbacks, Investing, Formulas, & Strategies

MEMO 12

Wealth Budget Planner

Monthly Overview

Month: Yr:

Income	Amt.		Income	Amt.	
					Add totals A & B to calculate your total monthly income
Total A		+	Total B		=

Expense	Amt.		Expense	Amt.	
					Add totals C & D to calculate your total monthly expenses
Total C		+	Total D		=

Monthly Income - Monthly Expenses	-
Discretionary Income	

Increase your discretionary income by reducing expenses, or generating more income. It is key to saving, investing, and being financially free.

Spend less than you earn and do more with less.

Monthly $100\left(\frac{\text{Expenses}}{\text{Monthly Income}}\right)$	$100\left(\frac{\quad}{\quad}\right)$
Debt To Income Ratio %	

Aim for a debt to income ratio of less <36%. This ratio is an indicator of your default risk. The lower the better.

Bill Tracker

Month: Yr:

Bill	Amt. Due	Due Date	Amt. Paid	Paid Date	Paid On Time
					Yes No
					Yes No
					Yes No
					Yes No
					Yes No
					Yes No
					Yes No
					Yes No
					Yes No
					Yes No
					Yes No
					Yes No
					Yes No
					Yes No
					Yes No
					Yes No
					Yes No
					Yes No
					Yes No
					Yes No
					Yes No
					Yes No
					Yes No
					Yes No

Calendar

Month: Yr:

	Sunday	Monday	Tuesday	Wednesday	Thursday	Friday	Saturday
Save Invest Build							
Dream Plan Live							
Save Invest Build							
Dream Plan Live							
Save Invest Build							

Notes & Reminders

Special occasions, Items to buy, Appointments, & To Do Lists

Wealth Budget Planner

Weekly Spending Tracker

Wk.#

/ / S M T W TH F S	
Add all columns for Daily Total:	

/ / S M T W TH F S	
Add all columns for Daily Total:	

/ / S M T W TH F S	
Add all columns for Daily Total:	

/ / S M T W TH F S	
Add all columns for Daily Total:	

Wealth Budget Planner

Weekly Spending Tracker

Wk.#

/ / S M T W TH F S	

Add all columns for
Daily Total:

/ / S M T W TH F S	

Add all columns for
Daily Total:

/ / S M T W TH F S	

Add all columns for
Daily Total:

/ - / Week End Totals

Sun.	
Mon.	
Tues.	
Wed.	
Thurs.	
Fri.	
Sat.	
Week Total:	

How much did you save this week?

Is there extra to invest?

List your week total and money saved on the monthly budget tracker.

Think of ways to cut back on unnecessary spending, or how to spend more efficiently.

Wealth Budget Planner

Weekly Spending Tracker

Wk.#

/ / S M T W TH F S	
Add all columns for Daily Total:	

/ / S M T W TH F S	
Add all columns for Daily Total:	

/ / S M T W TH F S	
Add all columns for Daily Total:	

/ / S M T W TH F S	
Add all columns for Daily Total:	

Wealth Budget Planner

Weekly Spending Tracker

Wk.#

/ / S M T W TH F S	
Add all columns for Daily Total:	

/ / S M T W TH F S	
Add all columns for Daily Total:	

/ / S M T W TH F S	
Add all columns for Daily Total:	

/ - / Week End Totals

Sun.	
Mon.	
Tues.	
Wed.	
Thurs.	
Fri.	
Sat.	
Week Total:	

How much did you save this week?

Is there extra to invest?

List your week total and money saved on the monthly budget tracker.

Think of ways to cut back on unnecessary spending, or how to spend more efficiently.

WEALTH BUDGET PLANNER

WEEKLY SPENDING TRACKER

WK.#

/ / S M T W TH F S	

ADD ALL COLUMNS FOR
DAILY TOTAL:

/ / S M T W TH F S	

ADD ALL COLUMNS FOR
DAILY TOTAL:

/ / S M T W TH F S	

ADD ALL COLUMNS FOR
DAILY TOTAL:

/ / S M T W TH F S	

ADD ALL COLUMNS FOR
DAILY TOTAL:

Wealth Budget Planner

Weekly Spending Tracker

Wk.#

/ / S M T W TH F S	
Add all columns for Daily Total:	

/ / S M T W TH F S	
Add all columns for Daily Total:	

/ / S M T W TH F S	
Add all columns for Daily Total:	

/ - / Week End Totals

Sun.	
Mon.	
Tues.	
Wed.	
Thurs.	
Fri.	
Sat.	
Week Total:	

How much did you save this week?

Is there extra to invest?

List your week total and money saved on the monthly budget tracker.

Think of ways to cut back on unnecessary spending, or how to spend more efficiently.

WEALTH BUDGET PLANNER

WEEKLY SPENDING TRACKER

WK.#

/ / S M T W TH F S	
ADD ALL COLUMNS FOR DAILY TOTAL:	

/ / S M T W TH F S	
ADD ALL COLUMNS FOR DAILY TOTAL:	

/ / S M T W TH F S	
ADD ALL COLUMNS FOR DAILY TOTAL:	

/ / S M T W TH F S	
ADD ALL COLUMNS FOR DAILY TOTAL:	

Wealth Budget Planner

Weekly Spending Tracker

Wk.#

/ / S M T W TH F S	
Add all columns for Daily Total:	

/ / S M T W TH F S	
Add all columns for Daily Total:	

/ / S M T W TH F S	
Add all columns for Daily Total:	

/ - / Week End Totals

Sun.	
Mon.	
Tues.	
Wed.	
Thurs.	
Fri.	
Sat.	
Week Total:	

How much did you save this week?

Is there extra to invest?

List your week total and money saved on the monthly budget tracker.

Think of ways to cut back on unnecessary spending, or how to spend more efficiently.

Wealth Budget Planner

Weekly Spending Tracker

Wk.#

/ / S M T W TH F S	
Add all columns for Daily Total:	

/ / S M T W TH F S	
Add all columns for Daily Total:	

/ / S M T W TH F S	
Add all columns for Daily Total:	

/ / S M T W TH F S	
Add all columns for Daily Total:	

Wealth Budget Planner

Weekly Spending Tracker

Wk.#

/ / S M T W TH F S	
Add all columns for Daily Total:	

/ / S M T W TH F S	
Add all columns for Daily Total:	

/ / S M T W TH F S	
Add all columns for Daily Total:	

/ - / Week End Totals

Sun.	
Mon.	
Tues.	
Wed.	
Thurs.	
Fri.	
Sat.	
Week Total:	

How much did you save this week?

Is there extra to invest?

List your week total and money saved on the monthly budget tracker.

Think of ways to cut back on unnecessary spending, or how to spend more efficiently.

Wealth Budget Planner

Monthly Budget Tracker

Subtract your week end totals from your discretionary income	
Discretionary Income	
Week 1.	
Week 2.	
Week 3.	
Week 4.	
Week 5.	
Surplus Cash:	

Savings
Add savings 1-5 for total savings
1.
2.
3.
4.
5.
Total Savings:

"Rule No. 1: Never lose money. Rule No. 2: Never forget rule number 1."

Warren Buffet

Budget Check

Are you spending more or less than planned for the month?

Are you happy with your surplus amount of cash?

Did you meet your savings goal for the month?

Are there expenses that could be reduced or eliminated, by a change in behavior?

Did you generate any extra income?

Think of some things you can do to increase your surplus cash and write them down.

Every month you should learn something new or perfect an existing skill, research assets to acquire, invest in stocks, and focus on creating income streams. Create a habit of success. Strike through all that apply during this month.

Researched Assets	Read a book	Perfected a skill
Invested in stocks	Thought of new income streams	Set new goals
Learned a new Skill	Wrote Down Ideas	Relaxed

....

....

....

If missed anything you wanted to do, be honest and write down what stopped you. Try your best to remove or change obstacles that stifle your success.

....

....

....

....

FINANCIAL STRATEGIES & CALCULATIONS

SAVINGS GOALS, CUTBACKS, INVESTING, FORMULAS, & STRATEGIES

Financial Strategies & Calculations

Savings Goals, Cutbacks, Investing, Formulas, & Strategies

WEALTH BUDGET PLANNER

SUCCESS IS WHAT YOU MAKE IT

This budget planner is dedicated to all of the motivated people that decided to turn their dreams into their reality. It is the first in the "Don't Dream It, OVBE It"series, because I believe understanding your finances is the cornerstone of success.

I hope tracking your finances has become second nature. Financial literacy is essential to being debt free, and having the ability to create your own opportunities.

With your finances organized, you can continue to save, invest, and spend more efficiently. To learn about some of my personal financial strategies, visit the Wealth Building Newsletter category of the OVBE Blogs.

As you continue on your journey to build wealth, be sure to plan for the worst, hope for the best, and remember success is what you make it.

Welcome to OVBE Nation!

Made in United States
North Haven, CT
05 November 2026

21772050R00124